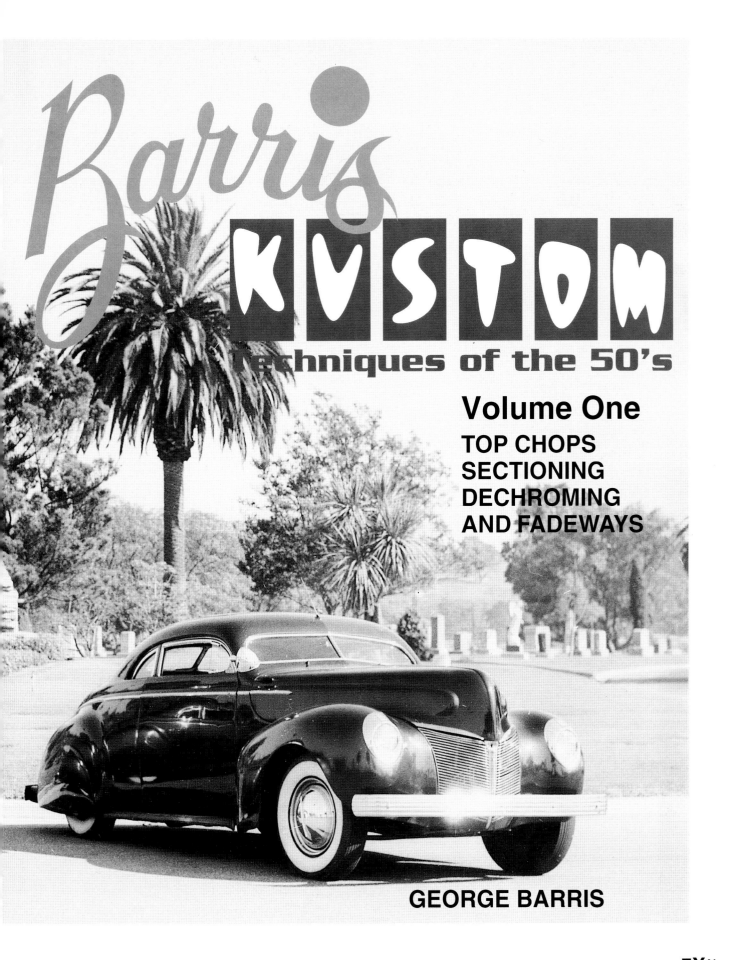

Barris KUSTOM
Techniques of the 50's

Volume One
TOP CHOPS
SECTIONING
DECHROMING
AND FADEWAYS

GEORGE BARRIS

First published in 1996 by Thaxton Press, PO Box 1742, Sebastopol, California. 95473 USA

The information in this book is true and complete to the best of our knowledge. All recommendations are made without any guarantee on the part of the author or Publisher, who also disclaim any liability incurred in connection with the use of this data or specific details.

We recognize that some words, model names and designations, for example, mentioned herein are the property of the trademark holder. We use them for identification purposes only. This is not an official publication.

Library of Congress Cataloging-in Publication Data Available
96-60751

ISBN 0-9652005-0-7

On the front cover: Lyle Lake's beautiful "Blue Danube" `52 Buick featured an unusual grille and bumper treatment, eyebrows over the headlights, a chopped top, and tri-tone paint.

On the frontispiece: Sam, on the left, and Johnny Zaro get through lifting the lid on Sam's `49 Merc. Last to go was this door frame. That's Johnny's convertible in the background.

On the title page: Two rarely seen `40 Mercs, left, Johnny Zaro's and, right, Al Andril's. Built in the late 1940s, both were subjected to typical Barris treatment: 5-1/2-inch top chop, channeled bodies, shaved handles and drip rails, filled seams, steel fender skirts, DeSoto bumpers and rear lights in the bumper guards.

Printed and bound in Hong Kong

Contents

Dedicated
To My Brother Sam

Introduction

Welcome to Barris Kustom Techniques, Volume One, the first in a series of four books which delve deeply into my personal photographic archives to visually explore how customs were built in their glorious, immediate post-war and early-1950s, golden age.

It should be noted that these books are not meant as a how-to guide for those building customs today. Materials, technology and methods have changed dramatically since we developed our skills, so rather than how to do it, these books depict how we did it back then, using our limited knowledge and the technology, such as it was, of the time.

Most of the photographs were taken at Barris Kustom of our own cars, the cars of those who worked for us, and customers' cars. However, a few of the vehicles included were built at other shops, recorded and included because of their significance.

Anybody who was there at the time will confirm that I always had a camera handy; there was a reason for this. I sold one-time rights for the use of these photographs to the fledgling Petersen Publishing Company, known then as Trend Inc., it and others published the material in dozens of magazines. The ensuing publicity drove our business, bringing us customers from as near as Hollywood and as far away as Florida, and helped make Barris one of the most recognized names in the automotive industry. Some of this material has therefore been seen before but not for 30 or 40 years. Where possible, we have tried to use photographs not previously published, making new prints from original, unused negatives.

In compiling these books, it was difficult to know how to arrange the contents. Ultimately, we decided to feature the customs by model year. It would be impossible to list them in any other way, since they often took years to build, and to be honest, nobody remembers exactly when we built what.

I'd like to take this opportunity to thank everybody who was involved at the time: my late brother Sam, to whom these books are dedicated; our staff; our customers; and the magazine editors who publicized our efforts. Thanks also to David Fetherston and Tony Thacker of Thaxton Press, who are publishing this series, Greg Sharp of NHRA Historical Services who acted as archivist, and Hershel "Junior" Conway, who filled some of the gaps in my memory. Hopefully, these books will be a guide and an inspiration to those of you who spell custom with a K.

George Barris

Acknowledgements:

Thaxton Press would also like to thank these wonderful folks: Teka Luttrell for his input on the design and layout. Paragon 3 in Santa Rosa, California, for their cover design work and at Fetherston Publishing, Gloria Fetherston and Nanette Simmons, at Simmons Editorial Services for their work on production.

As always, I had my camera at the ready. In the background were Dave Bugarin's '51 Merc, Frank Monteleone's '55 Ford, and Saint Vasquez' '49 Chevy—what a line-up.

Barris

Sacto and South

My brother Sam and I were born in 1924 and 1926, respectively, in Chicago, Illinois. In 1929 the family moved west to settle in Roseville, California, in the heart of the Sacramento Valley.

Though I won several prizes with model cars I had built, it was a dilapidated 1925 Buick that became our first real automotive project, with me bashing on the mangled fenders while Sam applied the paint—orange and blue, with diagonal stripes of various colors—shades of things to come, no doubt. Eventually, we sold the Buick and replaced it with a '29 A, which was outfitted with six antennas (though it had no radio), dozens of lights, fake supercharger pipes, winged ornaments, and a foxtail.

I was so intrigued with metal-shaping that I began spending all my spare time at a local body and fender shop. Eventually, the owner let me "set in" the license plate of a '36 Ford—a popular practice of the time.

Knowing even then that this was going to be my life, I started helping out, when I could, at Harry Westergard's Sacramento shop and bought a '36 Ford cabriolet. Over a period of time, I set in the license plate, installed teardrop taillights, lowered the car, removed the handles and installed

Right: Here's my '36 Ford convertible, with paint on the car. You can see the top which had been made by Hall of Oakland. What you can't see is a "set-in" license plate and frenched tear-drop taillights.

Below: My '36 Ford convertible was an ongoing project. At this point, I was working at Brown Brothers in Sacramento, where I had molded the lights and seams, chopped and lowered it, removed the handles, and fitted a '41 Packard Clipper grille, '34 Pontiac hood sides, and DeSoto bumpers.

push buttons, added ripple discs and fender skirts, and gave it a lacquer paint job. Eventually, it got a Packard Clipper grille, a so-called alligator hood, Pontiac side panels, and DeSoto bumpers.

In 1941, while I attended Sacramento College, Sam joined the Navy. I was turned down for the military and, so, applied to the merchant marine and was subsequently told to go to Los Angeles.

I never did get called to go to sea; I got a job at Jones's Body, Fender & Paint Shop on Florence and Main in Los Angeles, where I worked my way up to foreman. The customs you see in the accompanying photographs were typical of the work done at Jones's at the time.

In late 1944, I opened my own small shop on Imperial Highway in Bell. When Sam was discharged the following year, I persuaded him to join me in my venture despite his lack of experience. That was 1946, and we struggled until my '41 Buick won top honors at the first Hot Rod Show at the Los Angeles Exposition Armory. That really put us on the map. Consequently, we moved to new, larger premises at 7674 Compton Avenue.

Left: While waiting in Los Angeles to be called by the merchant marine, I got a job at Jones's Body, Fender & Paint Shop at Florence and Main. To begin with, they didn't do much custom work, but when they saw I could bring in that kind of business, they encouraged me, and it began to pick up. This rare (Ford only built 979 of them), chopped '40 Mercury convertible sedan and the other Mercury, beyond, were typical of the cars we built there.

Right: We quickly outgrew that first shop and, after winning top honors at the first Los Angeles Exposition Armory Hot Rod Show with my '41 Buick, we relocated Barris Kustom Automobiles for six months or so in late 1949 to 4120-1/2 E. Florence Avenue, Bell. There, we worked on this '42 Ford, which we chopped and channeled (you can see we're torching out the tunnel to clear the driveshaft) and rolled the running boards.

Right: This '38 Ford V8 coupe belonging to Dick Fowler was a typical early custom that was channeled and shaved with a chopped top, filled seams (we called it "sealed in" then), fender skirts, and a Packard grille. It was photographed outside the Compton Avenue shop.

Left: Early in 1950, we changed the name to Barris's Custom Shop and moved to 7674 Compton Avenue, Los Angeles. This Chevy, typical of the times, was one we had fitted with a '47 Olds grille and a top by Gaylord. We were also an official Brake Station which helped improve the the cash flow day to day.

Eventually, we outgrew the Compton Avenue shop and in 1949, moved to 4120-1/2 E. Florence Avenue, Bell. We were only in that shop for a short time, time enough to run a 1/2-page ad with Gaylord in the February 1950 issue of *Motor Trend*, then we moved within 6 months or so to 11054 S. Atlantic Boulevard, Lynwood, and that's when business really took off. We were working all hours of the day and night, and I look back now, feeling sorry for our neighbors who must have been driven crazy by our constant sawing, grinding, banging, and welding.

Those were wild and heady days. After all, we were just young guys having a good time cutting up what were often brand-new cars, and as you can see in the photographs that follow, we were not always taking the care we should have.

For example, Nick Matranga's beautiful '40 Merc met its fate in the hands of its new owner: wrapped around a telephone pole while street racing. Some, like Ron Guidry's tasteful '36 coupe, were destroyed in the fire of '57, while I was nearly decapitated, running under the back of a hay truck towing Dan Landon's '49 Chevy in

my '53 Lincoln.

Nevertheless, we had a lot of fun and I'm only thankful that I had the foresight to photograph much of what went on around the shop, for it is an amazing chapter in American automotive history.

Above: A typical day at the shop with all the guys goofing around, showing their strength, that's Red holding me up. In the background is my '41 Buick which, as you can see, is partway through the fadeaway treatment. More about that on page 32.

'36 Ford - Top Chop

The first cut is always the deepest. Here, after marking out the cut lines, Sam uses an air chisel to slice 4 inches out of the back quarter of this '36 three-window.

Moving to the front, notice that all glass has been removed prior to any cutting. Here, a hacksaw is being used to take 3 inches out of the A-pillar and the door frame. Both are cut at different points.

After slicing all four corners, Sam and Earl Harman, one of our prep guys, lifted the roof. Notice that the door frames remain uncut.

With the A-pillars clamped into position, the rear section of the roof was cut off in the middle of the door opening using a hacksaw and two tape lines as guides.

Here Sam uses a jack to support the front half of the roof as he carefully adjusts it into the correct position for welding.

When Sam had everything properly aligned and clamped into place, he gas welded the A-pillars first. Initially he just tacked them into place and later when he had aligned all the other new seams he came back and finished them off.

Again, using a jack to support the roof, the rear door pillars were welded in the door jam only.

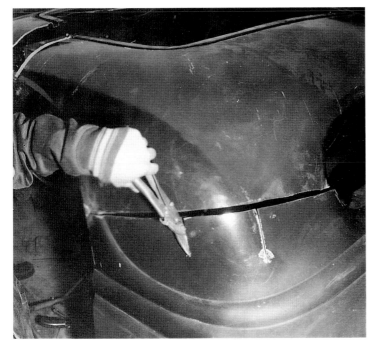

Here in the top left, you can see the gap created by the stretch and also the splices made in the rear quarter which enabled the roof panel to be massaged.

From the inside, you can see how Sam pulled the two halves of the roof together and hammer-welded the joint.

A strip of sheet metal was welded into the roof to fill the gap caused by the stretch. Also, a piece of scrap, cut from the portion of the door frame that was chopped, was used to fill the gap in the top of the door frame caused by the stretch.

With all welding completed, Sam used an angle grinder to finish off the new seam.

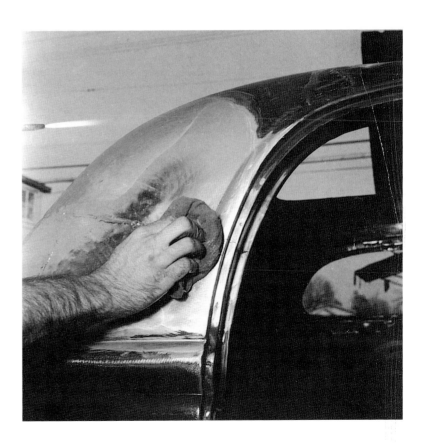

Finally, the area was given a liberal coating of lead which could be shaped to a smooth contour.

'36 Ford - Ron Guidry

December 7, 1957, is a day I'll never forget, when the Atlantic Avenue shop caught fire. I lost 14 cars that night, including Ron's coupe. The insurance company claimed "an act of God." Ron, from Long Beach, and a member of the Renegades, had worked on his car for 5 years.

Left: Figured it out? Well, it's an inverted `39 Nash grille mounted in custom-made side panels that were popular at one time. Under the louvered hood resided an ohv Olds with adjustable lifters, mag rockers, and a `54 Cad four-barrel carb. We chopped the top 2 inches in the front and 2-1/2 in back and molded `39 Ford taillights into the rear fenders.

Above: `39 Ford teardrops were mounted sideways and frenched into the fenders, which were "sealed in" as were the running boards fitted with MG rubber step strips. The bumper was a cut-down `51 Studebaker item. The pinstriping was by Art Summers of Santa Monica, though Dean Jeffries later added some abstract stuff.

Right: Ron`s car was in the shop for some minor reworking and a repaint when the place caught fire and the car was totally destroyed along with 13 others.

'39 Ford - Bruce Glenn

This was a Harry Westergard car built in the 1940s, when I was hanging out at his shop. I photographed it in 1953 and included it because it's a great example of his work and style which was such an influence on Sam and me. Bruce's '39 convertible, which hailed from Watsonville, California, embodied many features popular on pre-World War II customs. This work included adding a Packard grille, DeSoto bumpers, dechroming and molding the body, shaved handles, a removable steel hardtop, a "set-in" license plate, exhausts exiting through the fenders, teardrop taillights, and Cadillac hubcaps. Notice, also, that there is no opening trunk on this car.

Bruce Glenn's '39 convertible featured a Packard grille, DeSoto bumpers, dechroming and molding, shaved handles, and a removable steel hardtop.

Below: From the rear you can see the "set-in" license plate, exhausts exiting through the fenders and teardrop taillights. You can also see that Harry Westergard molded in the trunk to give this '39 an extra smooth look.

'40 Ford - Top Chop

Left: Here's Ralph Manok trial-fitting a filler panel into the chopped top of a '40 Ford. Back then, we called it "plating." Originally, we chopped the '40 much like we did the '36 shown on page 18. Eventually, however, we figured that by having these pre-formed panels made at California Metal Shaping, we could save time and do a much neater job.

Lower Left: You can see here that the panel has been shaped to fit a hole cut in the rear quarter of the roof. This technique negated the method employed earlier.

Below: The seam, however, still needed to be hammer-welded to provide a smooth join.

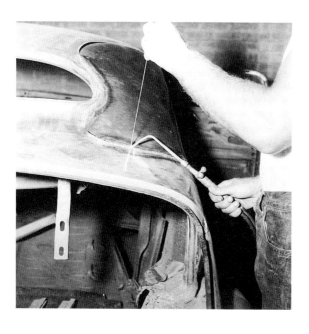

Right: Here in a corner of the shop given over to painting, you can clearly see all the bodywork, filled seams, shaved handles, and top chop, just prior to painting.

Above: To provide a good base for the lead, a sander was used to clean up the surface.

Above: Finally, a layer of lead was used to smooth out the whole area.

'40 Ford - Tom Hocker

Like so many customs of the time, Tom Hocker's '40 Ford would undergo constant changes and would soon feature quad, frenched headlights. However, it was an early full custom, having been started around 1948. Originally, we painted Hocker's '40 fuchsia orchid, but at the time these photographs were taken, it was painted in light metallic blue.

Although this looks like the '40 Ford on the previous pages, we chopped several, and here I am, applying some primer to Tom's car prior to its first fuchsia-orchid paint job.

Right: A lot of work went into Tom's chop, which was 2-3/4 inches in front and 3-1/2 in the rear. Notice that we also removed the drip rail and rounded the doors. Also, the windshield was raked and had its center post removed and replaced by V-butting the glass and sealing with plastic. The side panels of the front grille were removed and filled, as was the hood seam, and the bumpers, from a '49 Pontiac, were narrowed and had lights installed in the guards. The headlights were also frenched, an unusual treatment for this particular car. That's Tom on the left, standing in front of Dave Bugarin's car, and on the right is Herb Conway's '54 Merc. Herb is Junior's brother.

Above: In those days, a custom wasn't much unless the fenders were molded into the body. Tom's car had all that and more. It was channeled, shaved, had its cowl vent filled, and was radically lowered. The rear gravel pan was leaded into the body, and the car was fitted with fender skirts. The rear bumper was likewise fitted with handmade lights in the guards, while the exhaust exited through the ends.

'40 Ford - Hood Section

Left: This was Slim Messick's '40 Ford which had had the body channeled over the frame, necessitating the hood being sectioned. We usually did this right below a trim line, and, here, you can see that the trim has been removed and a cut line marked with tape.

Below: The sliced hood top was bolted back onto its hinges. Sam typically wore a Barris shirt and his goggles on his head.

Left: The hood was cut with our trusty air chisel. This separated the side panels so they could be attached to the body work.

Above: With the hood sides fixed into place, the hood top was cut along the trim line and the flaps pushed in.

Above: With the flaps pushed in, the hood top fitted inside the hood sides, and they, in turn, were trimmed to the trim line in the hood.

Here we see John Manok reworking the hood sides. He welded the top section to the side panels of the hood along the trim line, then ground and leaded it smooth.

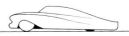

'40 Mercury - Nick Matranga

Undoubtedly, the quintessential chopped '40 Mercury club coupe was the one we built for Nick Matranga. Sam worked on it for over a year, perfecting the chop, getting it right when we had the idea of cutting the windshield opening up into the roof. The car was started at Compton Avenue but finished at Lynwood. Sadly, the car barely existed a year. Nick was in Korea and decided to sell it; early in '52, the new owner lost control on some railroad tracks during a rainy-night street race and wrapped it around a telephone pole. The driver walked, but the Merc was totaled.

Above: Nick's Merc always picked up a ton of trophies. Here in this rare shot from the '51 Oakland show, you can see how the front windshield was pushed up into the roof line. The top was chopped 5 inches; however, Nick would not let us change the front end of the car at all, except for the addition of a '46 Ford bumper.

Left: Hardtop styling was all the rage, so we cut out the door posts and made the chrome frames. The trim was basically stock but shortened in the hood section. All the fenders were molded, as was the gravel pan, the skirts were '41 Buick teardrops, and the taillights were replaced with handmade units in the bumper guards.

'41 Buick - Fadeway

Sam and I liked fadeaways, and they became one of our trademarks. Building a fadeaway into a car immediately set it apart and stamped it as a custom. Usually, we'd buy the panel from a Buick dealer—they weren't very expensive—and adapt them to whatever we were building, in this case, a '41 Buick convertible. It was relatively simple to do except for the front door opening. The conversion gave the car a whole new look with a smooth, rounded bodyline.

Right: Using a handy straight edge, the first thing we did was mark the door panel as to where we wanted the fadeaway. Here, we had to relieve the front fender so that the door would open.

Above: Here, you can see Ralph Manok adding a panel that goes between the outer skin and the bottom of the original door. We liked to work as much on the bench as possible to do this kind of work as it made for quicker, cleaner jobs.

Above: You can see three things in this shot: the fadeaway being trimmed to fit the contour of the door, original trim holes filled, and the front of the panel bent in so that it cleared the front fender. Finally, the fadeaway was tack-welded to the original door.

Above: Once the new fadeaway panel was tacked in place, it was possible to check the door opening clearance. This was a critical stage to doing this work but once you had it right the rest of the installation was straightforward.

Above: With the door on the bench, it was easier to lead the joint. Notice how we formed the fadeaway where it went into the front fender with a rounded leading edge. Leading was also a critical part of the work.

Above: Though not the Buick in the build-up, this is the `41 club coupe we did for Var Martin in the early days at Compton Avenue after I had built my Buick. It featured fadeaways, of course; a top chopped 3-1/2 inches in front, 5 inches in back; a `47 Cad grille; `47 Olds bumpers; and an interior by Runyan.

'41 Buick - George Barris

It's been so many years, it's hard to remember in exactly what order events occurred. However, I built this Buick while at the Compton Avenue shop, and it was one of many. Because it was such a great looking car it became very popular to customize it at the time. . . even Sam had one.

Above: Needless to say, the Buick attracted a lot of attention.

Left: This shot was taken at El Mirage dry lake, Muroc having been closed during the war. As you can see, the car was still in its early stages, with a white-primer finish, no top, and still plenty of work to do on those fenders and fadeaways.

Left: This is how the car was finished, as it appeared at the Los Angeles Exposition Armory show and on the cover of the May 1948 issue of *Road and Track*. Notice it now has a different bumper, with parking lights in the guards.

Left: The wreck gave me the opportunity to redo the car, and as you can see in these Don Cummins photographs shot on 76th Street next to our Compton Avenue shop, I'd fitted a `49 Cad grille.

Above: In this rear view you can see that the full fadeaways, filled seams and taillights mounted in the bumper guards, gave the car a clean look. Way over on the left of this photograph you can see yet another Buick we were working on.

Right: The crashed Buick. I wasn`t always as careful as I should have been. Oh well, it gave me a chance to do some more work.

'41 Ford - Jesse Lopez

Jesse Lopez of Bell, California, was a member of the Kustoms of Los Angeles car club that began the whole car-show thing with its impromptu gatherings in resorts like Balboa. Jesse eventually went into partnership with Junior; however, his club coupe was started in 1946 and completed two years later. He later sold the car to Danny Lares, who was the starter at Lions Drag Strip.

Above: Swapping Cadillac grilles was very popular, and Jesse's '41 was fitted with one from a '48. The bumpers were '47 Ford, fitted with '46 guards. The body was channeled and had its frame kicked up over the rear axle.

Right: By 1953 Danny Lares owned the car, and you can see his Road Kings, Wilmington, club plaque attached to the bumper.

Left: We chopped the top 4-1/2 inches, laid down the rear window, and removed the drip rail. Rear bumper is also '47 Ford, with '46 guards fitted with taillights to give the body a clean appearance.

'41 Ford - Frank Monteleone

In the January '57 issue of *Rod and Custom*, the editors described Frank Monteleone's '41 Ford convertible as the ultimate '41, and standing just 56 inches high, perhaps it was. It underwent a great deal of modification at a number of shops, Frank wanted his car updated with all the current styling trends. It wasn't finished until 1956 and we handled most of the finish work and the paint.

Above: Bent and chromed steel tube was used to fabricate the grille surround, which was filled with chromed steel mesh. The bumper is a modified '51 Merc. Extreme lowness was achieved by using a steeply "Dagoed" front axle and a de-arched spring up front and a Z'd frame in the rear.

Left: Frank stands proudly by his 7-year creation outside the Pan Pacific Auditorium. The tri-tone paint, charcoal metallic, shocking pink, and finishing white, supposedly predated Detroit by a number of years. Gaylord handled the interior with pink-and-white rolled and pleated Naugahyde. The headliner alone had more than 500 1-inch pleats. Stock taillights have now given way to recessed units from a '55 DeSoto. Notice, also, the exhaust tips which exit below and outboard of the '51 Olds bumper to prevent scraping. Swivel casters were used for the same purpose. Pan and fenders were all molded to the body.

Below: It's hard to tell this is a '41 Ford, since only the center section of the electronically operated stock hood remains, the outer edges being from a later-model Cadillac. The grille opening is from a '50 Mercury, while the headlights are '50 Olds.

Above: The use of Olds fenders necessitated the fabrication of full-length fadeaways which almost completely disguise the origin of the '41. Functional scoops in the rear fenders fed air to the rear brakes and hid the switch for the doors. Notice that the car had wires and knockoffs during this construction shot.

Below: All four original fenders were replaced with those from a '50 Olds, and the top, secured by quick-release catches, was fabricated from the top of a '38 Ford sedan. The electronically operated trunk lid is stock except for rounded corners. Notice that the taillights remain stock at this point.

'41 Mercury - Bill De Carr

Bill De Carr built this '41 Merc business coupe while he worked for us. Eventually, the car went to Dick Hansen in Sioux Falls, South Dakota, and consequently was never really featured in any magazines. The car was valued at $3,100 after a total of $2,400 worth of work.

Above: According to an old caption written on the back of this photograph, Bill chopped this car 4 inches; fitted it with a `48 Olds grille, push-button doors, electric windows; and painted it maroon.

Left: This great construction shot of Bill`s Merc, taken at the Compton Avenue shop, clearly shows all the work in channeling the body 5 inches, creating those fadeaways, molding the fenders, frenching the lights, and chopping the top.

'41 Ford - Anne De Valle

One of the many women into customs at the time was Anne De Valle. Her Ford was a classic and really looked the part with wide-whites, molded bodywork, a chopped top, Dodge hubcaps and frenched headlights. Sadly, her '42 club coupe was rarely featured in any of the contemporary magazines, which was a shame because it was a very nice car.

Above: The front end featured a '50 Olds grille and bumper under an extended hood, frenched headlights, filled seams, and foreshortened trim. Hood louvers were unusual for a custom but they indicate the changes taking place in the scene as owners constantly sought to modify their cars in their pursuit of show trophies.

Left: Notice how the bottom of the door had been extended to include the wraparound panel that replaced the running board. Door and deck handles were replaced with solenoids.

Below: The rear of Anne's car sported a '47 Buick bumper fitted with '46 Chevy taillights and plenty of pinstriping by Dean Jeffries. Notice also the side exhaust exiting just ahead of the rear fender.

'47 Buick - Don Vaughn

We first customized this '47 Buick Super convertible back in 1949 for Don Vaughn of Port Orchard, Washington. Don drove it for a couple of years and then brought it back to us to start on yet another round of modifications.

As you can see, it turned out to be a classic custom with its chopped Carson top, shaved bodywork, frenched headlights and fadeaway side panels. Don later sold it to Jim Collins of Gardena, California.

Above: This Buick's hood came in for a lot of work. We removed the stock outside latches and replaced them with pull latches hidden in the grille. We also recontoured the hood to make the lines converge in a point above the grille which, like so many customs, came from a '48 Cadillac, as did the front and rear bumpers. Notice that we moved the parking lights from the fenders into the grille.

Above: '48 Cad rear fenders had to be sectioned 3 inches to fit the Buick before they were filled and fitted with '52 Cad taillights. The bumper, however, is '48 Cad, fitted with neat little oval outlets for the exhaust. All trim was removed from the trunk lid, which was opened by a pull handle inside the car.

Right: In a shot taken sometime in 1953, Nick Matranga appears to be polishing the bumper of what was, by then, Jim Collins' Buick. We'd made the frame for the top before sending it over to Gaylord for covering. Gaylord also did the interior in two-tone leatherette. Interestingly, the car had a steering wheel and shift knob of clear plastic. The car was painted in purple-mist lacquer. In the background is Dale Marshall's Merc.

'46-48 Chevrolet -"High School Confidential"

We had long been attracting Hollywood stars to the shop, people like James Dean and Jayne Mansfield, and often this led to what would eventually become our core business, building movie cars. In 1956, we were approached by MGM, who was looking for two customs to be featured in a movie initially called "13 Hours of Terror" which eventually became "High School Confidential." We got the job to create the movie cars and purchased two clean, stock '46 Chevy coupes and proceeded to chop the tops 6 inches, shave and lower them, and install custom grilles and push-button doors. One of them was even fitted with a crude roll bar for the stunt scenes.

Lyle Lake is seen here, lifting the roof of the second car. The hood has already had its side trim shaved and its center seam welded.

Left: On the first car, you can see that John has removed the door and window frames, dropped the rear of the roof down, and tacked it to the body.

Right: The roof of the second car has likewise been chopped and dropped. Curly Hubert and Lyle are seen here, removing the rear quarter panels of the roof. You can see that the right side has already been removed.

John, using sheet metal cut to shape, is filling in the rear side
window. Notice the shape of the hole cut out for the new roof panel.

Here, Lyle is trial-fitting the left roof panel.   You can see
that the one on the right has already been tacked in place.

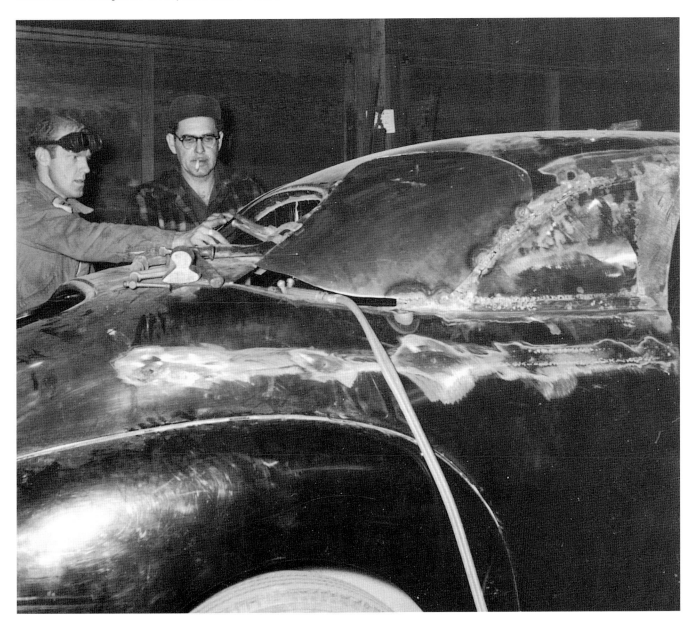

The cars caused plenty of interest when we took them for gas just
down the road from the shop. Notice the price, just 23.9 cents a
gallon for Golden Eagle regular. This shot also shows the custom
grille we installed using Ford, Chevy and Cadillac components.

Above: Despite the rush to get these cars built for the movie, their overall stance is quite pleasing and tough-looking. Notice that we removed the door handles but not the trunk handle nor the hinges.

Below: We had quickly learned that cars for the movies only needed to look the part and did not need the attention to detail required of a show car. Nevertheless, both cars, albeit only in primer, looked pretty good parked outside the shop.

'46 Ford - Pete Brock

Though Pete went on to become the designer of Carroll Shelby's Daytona Coupe, in his younger days, he was a hot rodder. He liked to call his '46 Ford convertible "El Mirage" a modern roadster, saying, "I don't like customs, they're lead barges." The custom work on the convertible was started in '46 by Art & Jerry, owners of an early custom shop, and they chopped, channeled and sectioned it, and reshaped the fenders. Pete's Ford was one of the few rods or customs of the time which had any graphics or stripes. Pete picked up his idea and color combinbation of a white body and blue stripes from Briggs Cunningham's Le Mans race cars. Pete had bigger challenges yet to come and sadly, he had to sell the car to pay for his tuition at Art Center College of Design.

Norm Crum of Norm's Auto Body, 8175 Melrose Avenue, Hollywood, handled much of the rebuild on Pete's car, which had been sectioned 5-1/2 inches and then channeled over the frame another 5 inches. To give the wheels clearance, the fenders were raised up and the openings reshaped. Norm formed the grille from two '51 Merc grille shells and hand-formed the nose, while the hood was formed from aluminum.

Above: Austin Healey taillights and a mix of arctic white-and-pearl paint applied along with U.S. international racing stripes added to the confusion of styles that indicate Pete's ultimate direction. The Carson-style top was chopped 3 inches.

Right: With the door open, you can get a clear view of the extreme channel and section job. Pete's sitting on a pearl-and-dark blue "pleat and roll" job handled by Dick and Dale's of Redwood City, California. The carpets were bright red.

'47 Cadillac - Tony Sestito

The Cadillac was viewed as the ultimate car, the one we all aspired to and one that couldn't be customized. Tony Sestito of Sacramento felt otherwise and took his '47 convertible to Bertollucci's for the full, yet subtle, treatment. Interestingly, Bertollucci replaced the Cad grille, which was so popular, with that from an Olds. This one touch gave the Cad a whole new look.

The entire front-grille assembly was discarded before the hood was shaved and extended to meet the modified '52 Olds bumper with a floating bar from a '53 Olds. The seal-beam headlights were deeply recessed into the frenched rim; adjustment was from beneath the fender.

Left: Unlike many customs which had later finned Cad fenders added, Bertollucci's kept the styling simple by adding '50 Ford lenses and routing the exhaust through the '51 Olds bumper. Notice the chrome beading between body and fender. Trunk lid and doors were operated by solenoid and dash-mounted buttons.

Below: The windshield was chopped 2-1/2 inches, and a new Carson-style top, featuring a Plexiglas wraparound rear window, was fabricated by Hall of Oakland. While the rear seat was upholstered, along with the rest of the interior, in pleated and rolled red-and-antique-white Naugahyde by Cuddles, a white canvas tonneau cover kept it hidden from view. Because of a mild lowering job, the front wheel openings were lipped and reshaped to allow the wheels, shod with '53 Caddy hubcaps, to turn. In the rear, '51 Mercury fender skirts were trimmed and reshaped to cover the wheel openings. Notice, also, that most of the original trim was removed.

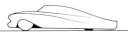

'47 Studebaker - Tommy Thornburgh

Tommy was another member of Kustoms of Los Angeles, and his family owned a Studebaker dealership in Huntington Park. Tommy was a rare customer to bring us this '47 Studebaker Champion convertible to customize. We charged about $165 to chop the windshield, $200 for the grille (including chrome), $150 for all the rear-fender work, and $15 to round each corner.

Above: To disguise the stubbiness of the '47 Studebaker Champion, we extended the headlight shrouds 2-1/2 inches. We also extended the hood down into the hand-formed grille opening, which featured a floating bar made from two '50 Lincoln grille bars mounted back-to-back with twin parking lights. The bumper was from a '52 Lincoln. Notice the original Stude air vents were filled and covered by '52 Pontiac side trim. Notice also, that Tom had the car up for sale here.

Left: Fender skirts aid the lengthening effect, as do '52 Stude taillights mounted horizontally in fenders which were filled and extended downward 2 inches. The rear bumper, with exhaust outlets in the bullets, was from a '52 Lincoln. Both rear and front gravel shields were welded and molded. The top, finished in dark royal blue, was built by Carson Top Shop to fit the 4-inch chopped windshield.

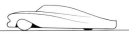

'49 Chevrolet - Marcia Campbell

Another woman interested in customs back in the early days was Marcia Campbell of Walnut Park, California, who was also a pretty good photographer and recorded many early customs. Marcia purchased the first convertible '49 Chevy to be delivered in the state of California and immediately brought it to Barris Kustom for the treatment. The car was sold the following year to Bill Chuck. Later, Marcia had Junior do her '56 Mercedes gullwing.

Above: This was the only shot we could find of the rear, so you'll have to look past the lovely Miss Temple City, Donna Greva, who is draped over the fender which was lengthened 4 inches, and raised 2 inches, and fitted with '50 Chrysler taillights. The rear bumper was a reformed '49 Olds part, and we relocated the gas filler inside the trunk. The door handles were shaved along with the trunk latch, to be replaced with solenoids. When Bill purchased the car, he installed a high-torque truck engine with Belond headers and duals.

Left: Lowering 3 inches in the front and 4 inches in the rear set the immediate stance for this clean custom, which had all of the trim removed and holes filled. As was often the case, we installed a cut-down and modified '49 Cad grille with frenched headlights, frenched and rolled gravel pan, and a bumper cut to fit. The padded top, to fit the 3-inch chopped windshield, was the work of Gaylord, who also installed the turquoise pleated interior.

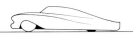

'49 Chevrolet - Dan Landon

Probably one of the nicest Chevys ever was Dan Landon's. Though simple in appearance, it hid an enormous amount of work because of the way we sectioned the top 2-1/2 inches before chopping it 5 inches. Dan was also a racer, hence the lack of a back seat, and his car featured a racy engine.

To achieve a low top while retaining reasonable window openings, we sectioned the roof of Dan's car 2-1/2 inches just above the tops of the doors before chopping the top 5 inches in front and 7 inches in the rear. The one-piece windshield from an Olds 88 was also let up into the roof, while the rear was given one of our so-called tapering swoops. The drip rail was removed, and the corners of the doors rounded. Notice, also, the subtle fadeaway. The side trim was from a Packard. The beautiful rear fenders were extended 8 inches and fitted with Frazer taillights. The exhaust tips were extended through the rear bumper, which came from an Olds 98. The trunk lid, like the doors, was operated by solenoids. Note, also, that we removed the beading from around the belt line, which was a tremendous amount of work but to great effect.

Above: The frame around the grille was made from 2-inch tubing before being fitted with bars from a Frazer and teeth from a DeSoto. The bumper was from a Pontiac. The hood was shaved and filled, while the headlights were frenched. To get the car low, we lowered it 4 inches in the front and 7 in the back by kicking the frame up over the rear axle, which necessitated rebuilding the floor of the trunk.

Right: Dan and I were returning from Sacramento when his engine blew, so we hooked his car to the bumper of my '53 Lincoln Capri. Coming over the Grapevine into Los Angeles in the fog, I ran into the back of a hay truck, and this was the result. The Lincoln came off much worse than Dan's Chevy. Within the year I had turned the Lincoln into the Golden Sahara, my first radical custom.

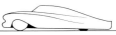

'49 Ford - Buster Litton

We originally chopped this '49 club coupe for its previous owner; then, Buster purchased it part-finished and took it to George Cerny of Compton, California, for the rest of the work.

I merely photographed the car as one of the best examples of the customized Ford shoebox. Incidentally, Buster sold the upholstery out of this car to Hershel "Junior" Conway.

Above: To complement the front rake, Cerny added '51 Olds 98 fenders with the stock taillights. The bumper was also stock, but its ends were replaced with those from a '53 Ford to give the necessary wraparound length. Note that all seams were filled, but the stock side trim was retained while all handles were removed.

Above: George Cerny made the transformation in just 6 months, finishing off the chop, removing the door posts, and adding the nose section from a '51 Merc, along with the front half of '51 Studebaker fenders, complete with headlights and trim reworked to include turn signals. The bumper was stock but relieved of all trim, while the gravel pan was fully molded. The hubcaps were '53 Cad.

Right: A bold step was taken in removing the door posts, but the hardtop treatment really works. Here, you can see Buster sliding the rear side glass into its channel. Glass from a Ford convertible was used in the doors. The interior, completely rolled and pleated, was the work of Gaylord.

'49 Mercury - Sam Barris

As soon as it was available, Sam bought a new '49 Merc and drove it every day until he figured out how to chop it. He immediately knew that the Merc would make a great looking custom but wanted to get his ideas sorted out before he started working on the car. In doing so, he created the classic custom car which today is still the most emulated custom design. Sam's Merc went on to win at the Second Annual National Roadster Show in Oakland. This was a very new look at the time and folks went crazy over it. Sam had numerous offers for the Merc right there on the floor of the show. He eventually let the car go to Bob Orr of Muscatine, Iowa.

In this build-up photo, Johnny Zaro attacks the rear of Sam's Merc. You can see how we used anything handy, exhaust pipes, whatever, to hold the roof up while we made the hacksaw cuts. This phase of getting the Merc chopped took many months but the end result was a great looking custom and the knowledge of how to do it right.

Right: The shaved trunk lid was operated by solenoids, as were the doors. Hand-made taillights fit almost flush with the fenders. The car was photographed by Marcia Campbell at the Lynwood Community Center.

Below: The extensive list of modifications included a 4-inch top chop, a 4-inch channel, full fadeaways, a shaved drip rail, rounded doors, shaved handles, frenched headlights, and a handmade spring-mounted, floating-bar grille.

'49 Mercury - Jerry Quesnel

By the time Jerry Quesnel brought his '49 Merc to us, Sam had chopping Mercs down to an art.
He had the window openings perfect, with the right amount of angle in the B-pillar and the rear quarter window scaled just right. Jerry's '49 turned out to be one of the cleanest and lowest Mercs ever built. With just two inches of ground clearance, this car looked like it was glued to the road. We eventually painted it in ruby, maroon and purple lacquer. Jerry later owned a nice '52 Ford.

Above: This rear 3/4 shot of the build up of Jerry Quesnel's '49 Merc shows the rear was completely shaved, and the taillights, which we made from plastic, were moved to reside in the bumper guards. The gas filler was moved inside the trunk, and all seams were molded.

Left: In this build up shot, Sam stands proudly by Jerry's white-primered ride. White, and eventually tinted, primer was very popular in those days. Extreme lowness necessitated cutting into the body to allow clearance for driveshaft, rear end, and running gear. Notice how Sam has put a radical lean on the door post and rounded the corners.

Below: With Jerry's and Sam's cars both out on the street, a chopped Merc suddenly became the quintessential custom car. The Merc also featured spots, white walls and Cad hubcaps, which today are almost mandatory custom accessories.

Above: This front 3/4 photo of Jerry's Merc shows all the front seams were molded and the grille opening smoothed out before the fabricated grille bar was mounted on springs and rubber mounts. Doors and trunk were solenoid-operated.

'50 Buick - Sam Barris

Most of the chopped fastbacks of the time had a nasty hump in the roof line, but when Sam chopped his sedanette, he got it right by removing 7 inches from the rear of the roof and sectioning the deck lid to match. For some reason, and I don't know why, I didn't take many build-up photographs, even though it took him almost two years of spare-time work to complete. Sam had bought the car from a wrecking yard after it had been gutted in a garage fire, and when it was all over, he said he'd never do another for himself that required so much work.

Left: In this rear 3/4 build up photo you can see that Sam has already chopped the top 3-1/2 inches and sectioned the rear of the body 5 inches, from a point below the rear of the quarter windows to the rear body panel, a chore that took several months to complete, and has begun extending the rear fenders and trying different taillight combinations.

Right: Here, you can see that the right-hand fender has already had its `54 Pontiac station-wagon taillight installed, while the left fender is stock. The fenders were also extended downward.

Above: Beautiful lines were accentuated by reversed '51 Lincoln trim, mounted upside down, and handmade skirts. The trunk handle was replaced with a solenoid, as were the door handles with the actuating buttons located in the lower door.

Right: Sam leaned back an Olds curved windshield and removed the drip rails to achieve a very clean look to this Buick. Incidentally, the drip rail was relocated inside the door opening. The headlights were frenched '53 Buick units and the floating grille was from a '53 Olds, with airscoops to direct air to the interior. The bumper was '53 Lincoln, and the hubcaps were '53 Cadillac. The bottle on the hood was our new Barris Kustom Kolor Glaze polish.

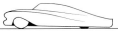

'50 Ford - Dechroming

Something we all tried to do in the early days was remove excess chrome trim; however, as the show thing gained momentum, builders started putting it back with a vengeance. One time, I remember

Sam did a deal with Junior where he would shave Junior's car and Junior would paint his house. Well, Sam had the hood done in less than a day, but it took Junior a lot longer to paint the house.

Above: Sam started by removing the original trim strip from this '50 Ford hood by unbolting it from the inside.

Below: Sam liked to be involved with his work and it was typical of him to climb up on the hood to grind away excess paint.

Below: In the next step, an electric drill and rotary brush were used to clean the area around the trim holes.

Above: The holes which were to be filled with braze were tapered with a drill; others were sealed with rivets.

Below: After filling, the area was well tinned before lead was liberally applied.

Above: Lead was kept soft with heat and pushed around with a well-oiled oak paddle. The lead was then ground and smoothed and readied for primer.

'50 Mercury - "The Twins"

This '50 Merc belonged to two guys known only as "The Twins" and as you can see, it was set to be a radical job, being chopped and sectioned. Sadly, I don't know what happened to the car.

We completed the section, put it back together, and got it into primer before the twins took it away, and that was the last we saw of it.

This group-shot in the workshop shows (left to right) Frank Sonzogni, Junior, Slim, and Dale Bird from the fire department, who used to hang out at the shop. Each time we sectioned a car, everyone would look at us in disbelief that we could chop up a perfectly good automobile. These guys loved doing this work and even they were amazed that we had sectioned the twins' Mercury. You can see clearly that we sectioned that car along the body crease line. This project happened in '55 or '56.

Right: This front 3/4 photo of their '50 Merc featured a sectioned pancake hood with rounded corners and more scoops than a Baskin-Robbins. The windshield was to be a wraparound from a '55 Chevy. One of the unusual features of this Merc was how the roof was to overhang the front glass. It gave the car a different yet crisp look.

Below: With those '49 -'50 Lincoln bolt-on eyebrows over the wheels, it looked like a Mercedes sports car. It's a pity that the car left our shop after being put into primer; we never saw it again. It sure turned out to be an interesting looking custom with its own unique touches including a curl in the upper edge of the side window opening.

'50 Mercury - Frank Sonzogni

The April '55 issue of *Rod and Custom* referred to Frank's '50 Merc club coupe as "The 730-Day Custom," because that's how long it took him to build it. The reason being, he had a day job as a police officer in Lynwood, California, when he wasn't busy working in our shop. Frank went on to be Junior's body man for almost 30 years. The car went to Arizona and was destroyed by fire.

Left: Sadly, there aren't too many build-up shots; nevertheless, here's Frank trying the angle of the raked door post. You can also see where he's removed the drip rail and welded the window frame back to the roof panel, which was lowered 3-3/4 inches.

Right: Because it was uncuttable tempered glass, the rear window retained its stock shape and size; however, it was laid down, and the roof was made to fit. Here, you can clearly see the various cut lines.

Above: The long hours were rewarded with a beautiful swooping taper to the roof. Notice the tape line for the fadeaways and the fact that Frank has already installed '51 Merc rear fenders.

Right: It was great working with people like Frank. Talented and creative people feed information back and forth and so you all discover new ideas and techniques. Frank's talent for perfect bodywork was memorable and here you can see him paddling the lead to cover all those stretch marks.

Above: Frank and his son Ed squat to show the swooping fadeaway, which tapered into '51 rear fenders extended by 9-1/2 inches and fitted with '54 Olds taillights. At one time, Frank had a series of '49 Ford dash knobs around the lights. The bumper was a '52 DeSoto item fitted with bumper guards and rectangular exhaust outlets. Small casters were used to prevent driveway scraping.

Right: The side trim was from a '53 Dodge, and the functional scoops were decorated with '53 Chevy 210 trim strips. Frank even built the hubcaps himself, using accessory caps fitted with a Ford grille spinner. Inside, the interior was handled by Bill Gaylord and featured a set of green-and-white dash knobs made by Bob Hirohata.

Right: Frank used '53 Ford headlight rims frenched into the fenders, and the grille features a '54 DeSoto assembly above a '52 DeSoto bumper. Notice the hood has rounded corners and the neat double layer pinstriping which frames the upper edge of the grille opening. The Merc's extreme lowering was achieved by chopping and reworking the A-arms in the front and then adding 4-inch lowering blocks in the rear, as well as a 6-inch stepped frame.

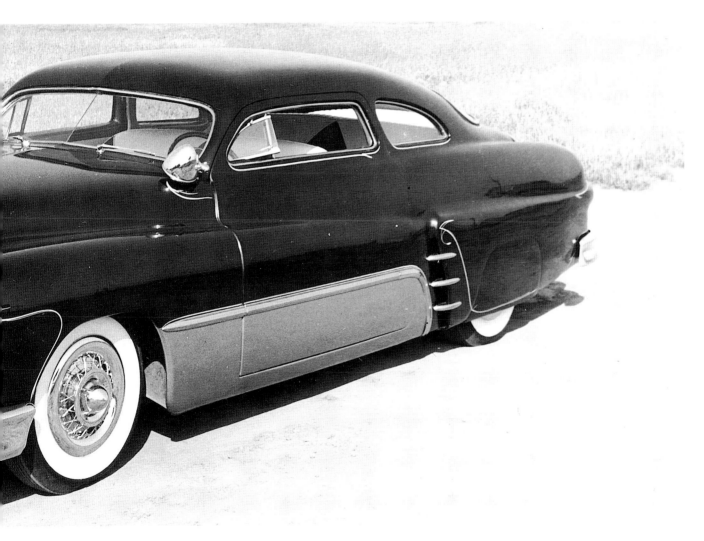

'50 Oldsmobile - Jack Stewart

Jack Stewart's "Polynesian," a '50 Olds 88 Holiday coupe built at Neil Emory and Clayton Jensen's Valley Custom in Burbank, was, without doubt, one of the most beautiful sectioned cars ever. The Polynesian featured on the cover of *Hot Rod Magazine* and was always a big attraction at the car shows. Even though these Ralph Poole photographs have been seen before, they graphically show how the section job was performed.

Above: This build up photo of the Polynesian shows that the top was not chopped but a 4-inch section was taken out of the car before the two halves were welded back together. Prior to any cuts being made however, Neil began by checking panel contours with a plumb line to find the widest spot on each. You can see on the doors, for example, how this point moved up and back. These coordinates were needed so that when the body was cut, the two halves would match up again. To mark the cuts, a long strip of 4-inch-wide aluminum was used as a template. In some places where panels were fairly vertical, like the rear fender, the cut was vertical.

Above: Emphasis was on clean, uncluttered lines expressed by a shaved hood, a simple grille with a wraparound bumper, and frenched lights. Perforations in the headlight rims, repeated in the fender scoops and rear lights, ducted air into the interior. The front wheel wells were opened up to allow for turning clearance, while the rears were covered with hand-formed skirts.

'50 Oldsmobile - Tom Davis

Tom Davis from Los Angeles liked to race, and he took this '50 Olds custom through the traps and across the dry lake of El Mirage at a very credible 112 mph. For some reason, the car was rarely featured. These photographs, taken around 1951, show the car with the top chopped but the grille yet to be installed.

Above: All handles were removed and the fenders were extended and fitted with the lower half of a '52 Cad taillight. Notice how the rear window of this car was not laid down as usual but, instead, was replaced with a much smaller, probably Plexiglas, window.

Above: Tom Davis's '50 Olds was chopped, had frenched headlights, and would later be fitted with a '53 Olds grille bar. Like many customs in the mid-fifties this Olds was done over a period of time as the owner continued to drive it on the street. Notice, also, that the hood has had the seam welded, the grille opening has been reformed and only some of the side body trim has been removed.

'51 Chevrolet - Larry Ernst

Larry's tale is a strange one. He was a priest in the Roman Catholic church and eventually became a Monsignor; that's why his name and the photographs with the model were rarely used in any of the contemporary articles. Larry loved cars and delighted in his Chevy. This car turned out to be one of the classic kustoms of the fifties, remembered by many people. We did the car twice for Larry, and he drove it out to Los Angeles both times from his home in Toledo, Ohio.

Above: Sam stands alongside his handiwork outside my little office on Atlantic Boulevard. You can see the rear fenders were extended(12 inches), raised (2 inches), and extended on the lower edge(1-1/2 inches) before being fitted with `50 Ford taillights and skirts.

Left: Here, you can see where we lengthened and molded the hood into one piece and installed a `51 Olds windshield in a frame that was both chopped and slanted 2-1/2 inches. The grille was formed from a Canadian Ford Meteor, and at this point, it still had the Chevy bumper.

Above: Here, we've yet to install the grille, but you can plainly see that we extensively reshaped the opening. You can also see those "back East" half-moon chrome headlight covers, combination Chevy and Olds trim, and a bumper midway through modification.

Left: Continental kits were another "back East" fad and, for Larry, we made up the gravel pan and molded it to the body. We also installed the spare on a bracket that allowed it to swing down so the trunk could be opened. We have yet to run the exhaust through the bumpers.

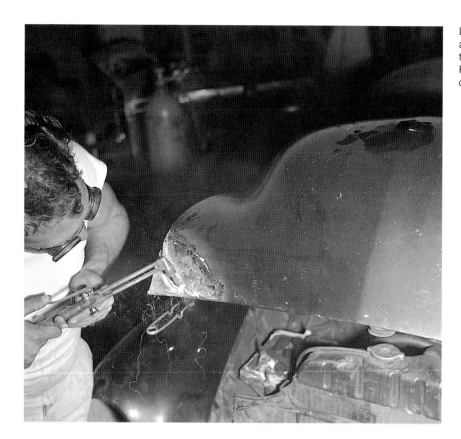

Left: Larry brought the car back out from Ohio and had us install scoops in the rear fenders, alter the taillights, and round the corners of the hood. Firstly, we marked out the radius and then torched off the corner.

Right: To refashion the body side of the rounded corner conversion, a piece of sheet metal was cut and formed to shape and then welded in to make the new corner.

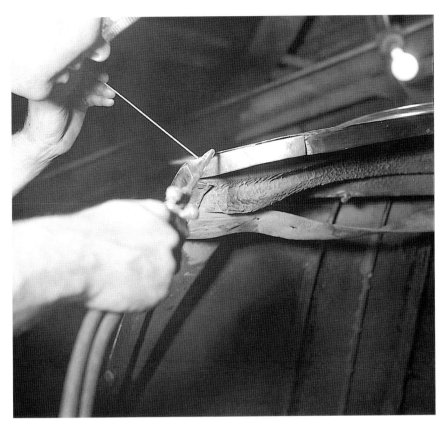

Left: Two pieces of sheet metal were cut to form the channel sides of each corner. These were gas welded into place and then ground smooth before being leaded.

Below: A liberal coating of lead was used to cover the new work and give the rounded corner its final shape before it was prepared for final finish and painting.

Above: Tommy Thornburgh, owner of a great-looking '49 Studebaker, is seen here, polishing Larry's car for a show to be held the next day in Pasadena, where it took a top award. The car was back on the West Coast for further modifications and you can see that the new side trims have not been fitted or the paint redone yet.

The final time around we changed the side trim, added a three-tooth scoop to the rear fenders, rounded the hood corners, and installed the bumper guards on a Pontiac bumper. By this time it also had two-tone paint and polished Cad hubcaps. Larry was delighted with the new look.

'51 Ford - Sectioning

As Detroit began to build slimmer bodies, the trend for sectioning faded. It was also a difficult and costly exercise that only a few customers would step up for. When this '51 Ford came to us, it was almost brand new and the owner had dreams of creating a wild kustom. We gutted the Ford and then sectioned it, but the owner never came back to give us any money to complete the job. The car sat outside the shop and after two years we hauled it to the junkyard.

Left: The '51 Ford offered a perfect canvas for the art of sectioning due to its fairly straight sheet metal and the horizontal trim line which provided the perfect place to cut.

Below: Sectioning any vehicle is time consuming and difficult. To make it easier we removed the front sheet metal and most of the firewall-mounted components before initial cuts were made.

Above: The firewall sectioning is taken at its base just above the footwells. However, to clear the steering column and the transmission hump the sectioning cut was made above both of these.

Above: At the rear, it was planned so that the trunk lid could be cut at its lower edge; we stayed above the splash pan.

Above: The doors could be done in several ways: section the door, as we did here, grind off the whole panel, and make a new one; or, buy a replacement panel, and cut it down.

Above: When all the body panels were cut, it was time to cut the support members. As you can see, we torched them in this case.

Above: Once we had cut all the body panel sections out evenly around the car we had to do the same thing to the interior structure of the car. To cut this structure away we would torch them or use a hacksaw or powersaw.

Above: Finally, the top half was lowered over the chassis. The seam was either hammer-welded or riveted together, and the join disguised by the original trim.

'51 Mercury - Bob Hirohata

Undoubtedly, the most famous custom of all time was Bob Hirohata's '51 club coupe, a canvas on which everything we had learned came together harmoniously and in only a few months. Soon after completion, Bob dropped in a Cadillac engine and drove the car non-stop from Los Angeles to Indianapolis for a car show. The story of his trip, in the October 1953 issue of *Rod and Custom*, is worth reading. The car is still around and is being restored by its current owner.

Above:To get that perfect roof line, a "tapering swoop" as I called it at the time, the top was chopped 4-inches in the front and 7-inches in the back. The door post was removed and new frames were made from 5/8-inch channel; however, they did not roll up with the windows. In profile, everything fell into place, the shaved handles, the fadeaway, the `52 Buick Riviera side trim "spear" dividing the two-tone paint, and the functional scooped fenders with flush `51 skirts. The taillights were `52 Lincoln, frenched low into the fenders.

Left: The filled and peaked hood, which extended down into the grille, had rounded rear corners to match the doors and deck lid, while the parking light surrounds were handmade from `50 Ford parts and chromed. The grille opening was likewise handformed and featured a handmade floating bar. The headlights are frenched and used the chrome rim from a `52 Ford.

'51 Mercury - Dave Bugarin

Dave Bugarin of San Pedro, California, was inspired to customize his '51 after seeing Bob Hirohata's Merc at the '53 Motorama. He didn't want us to copy Bob's car but rather create a new custom that had the same style and elegance. Dave didn't have a lot of money, so we worked on his car when he could afford it and the car was eventually finished after about two years. We began with the roof chop, which was subjected to an unusual treatment.

We selected a set of '53 Buick headlights for the front of the Merc. These we frenched into the fenders. Next we handformed the floating-bar grille from sheet metal and colored it satin blue. These little details helped give the Merc its own strong character and style.

Above: On Dave's car, rather than chop the roof off first as usual, we removed the B-post and the door frames first. This gave a much clearer view of what shape we wanted the new side window opening to be.

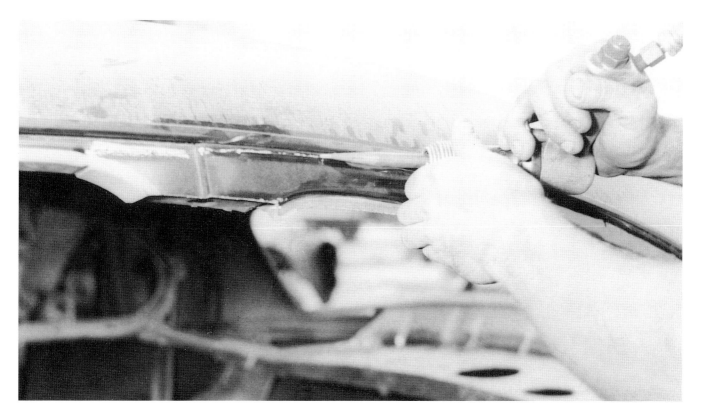

Above: Using an air chisel, we next removed the frames below the drip rail.

Below: Now the roof was removed completely. Notice here that the car had been fitted with a Cadillac grille. The car was a mild custom when Dave brought it to us.

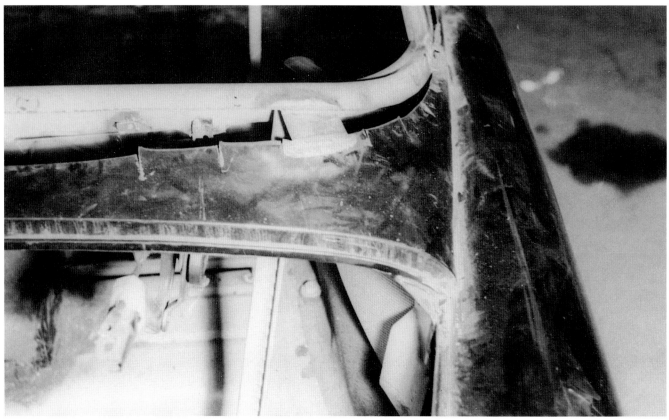

Above Left: Here, the rear window has been separated from the roof, while the roof itself has been welded back on at the front after 3-inches were cut from the A-pillars. The rear glass could not be cut and had to be laid down.

Above: A whole new rear cowl panel was made and welded into position. It was far easier to create a new section of sheet metal than to try to re-use the old section.

Left: After the rear bulkhead was sectioned, the window was tacked into position; and, because it was being laid down, the rear cowl was sliced and bent out of the way.

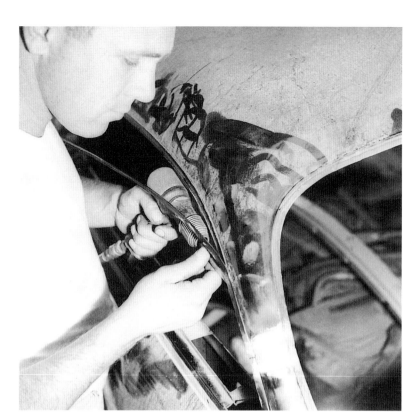

Left: An air chisel was used to remove the drip rail that remained on the front portions of the roof.

Below: To make the windows really narrow, we welded the top of the door frames to the roof. This gave the side windows a smaller look, making the chop look extreme.

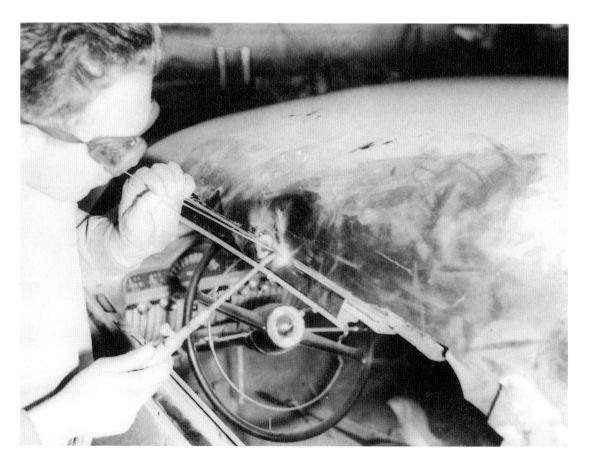

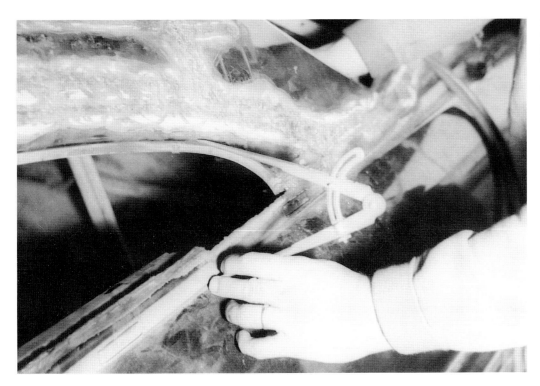

Left: Careful measurements were taken so as to make both sides the same. Notice the cuts and welds made to reshape the roof and accommodate the laid-back rear window.

Left: The top of the doors and the lower edge of the side windows were welded and leaded smooth.

Right: You can see here, clearly, how the door frame has been welded to the A-pillar, and the separation between the top of the door and the pillar.

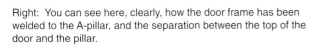

Right: Rotary files were used to finish off the tight corners of the side windows.

Below: New window frames were made from metal channel.

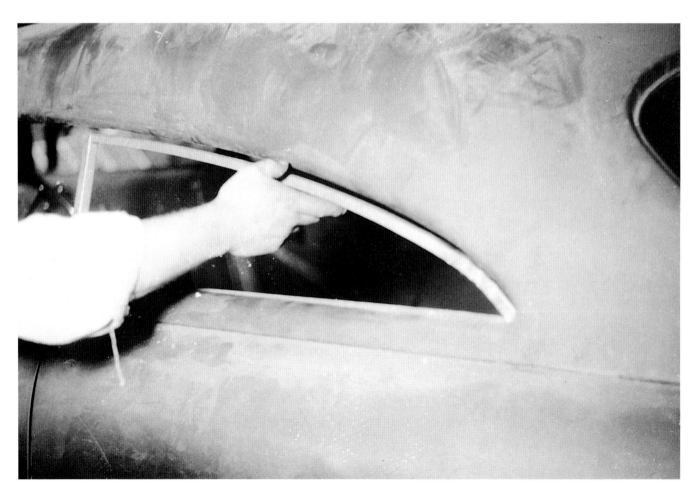

Right: This is how we extended the front of the hood. Sheet metal was rolled to shape and welded to the leading edge of the hood.

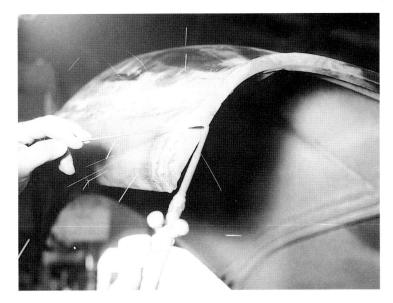

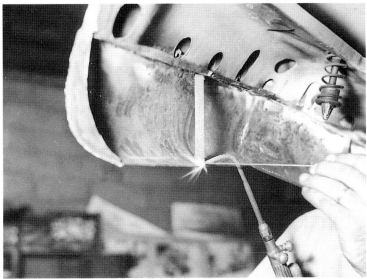

Left: Small brackets of strap steel were welded between the old hood and the extension.

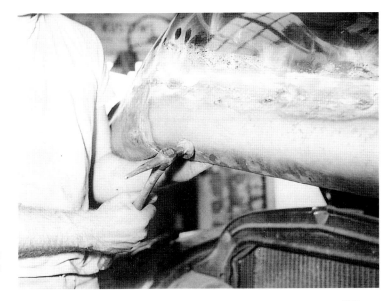

Right: The extended hood was hammered into shape before leading. We only performed this modification on a few cars, including the Hirohata Merc and Ralph Testa's.

Above: Finally we had the Merc finished in primer and almost
done— roof chopped, front glass in, window frames made, and we're
trying the side trim, which didn't finish up quite how it appears in this
photograph.

Below: Dave, like many of our customers, had a small problem with another car, and, here, you can see the damage to the door, trim, and fender skirt.

'52 Buick - Lyle Lake

Lyle Lake's '52 Buick, the "Blue Danube" was featured on the cover of Trend Book 143 - *Restyle Your Car*. The Buick was used to illustrate a story about typical customizing costs. The Buick is also featured on the cover of this book. Lyle moved out from Florida and became shop foreman for us. I managed to get his car into an episode of the TV show, The Twilight Zone.

Above: The top of Lyle's Buick was chopped 3 inches in front and 6 inches in the rear to achieve that pleasing slope. The headlights, which had dozens of little holes drilled in the rims, were shaded using accessory shades from California Custom Accessories. The grille opening was accented with aircraft tapered tubing and bumperettes made from '51 Chevy parts welded to Cadillac bullets. Later, the grille bars gave way to a drawer handle grille. The grille was made up from lengths of exhaust tubing and notice how the hood corners had been rounded into the tubing. To the right, you can see the abandoned '51 Ford that we had sectioned.

Above: As you can see, we're playing with trim ideas here. Eventually, we settled on Buick trim, used in conjunction with straight chrome trim that runs from the middle of the door all the way to the rear '53 Olds bumper fitted with exhaust exits.

Left: The main body color was pearl blue, while the top was sky-blue metallic and the bottom an ocean-blue mist. Dean Jeffries handled the white-and-copper striping. The rear scoops were functional and featured two chrome teeth. The fender skirts were later removed.

'52 Oldsmobile - Jack Nethercutt

Sixteen-year-old Jack Nethercutt came to us to customize his Olds Holiday 98. Jack wanted it chopped but chopping hardtops such as the Olds was difficult because of the wrap-around rear window. We figured it out and turned the Olds into an unusual and elegant custom. The car was known sometimes as the "Goldsmobile" because of its extensive use of gold plating, though its real name was "Viennese." It was later sold to Ronnie Smith of El Cajon, California.

Left: This build up photo shows the Olds with much of the bodywork done and in primer and the roof half chopped. Here, John Manok and I are lowering the roof back into position before welding the A-pillars.

Below: In this rear 3/4 photo you can see that the rear fenders were extended before the stock taillights were frenched. The side trim is a combination '53 Dodge and '53 Ford. The Olds also had square exhaust outlets in the bumpers and backup lights in the guards.

Above: At the front we used exhaust tubing to mold the new grille opening before installing a floating bar using the center section from a '53 Ford. The headlights, with scoops, were frenched, and the gravel pan was molded in. The bumper guards were taken from a '53 Mercury.

Right: The Olds got mangled in the rear quarter in another mishap. So Jack brought it back to us for repairs. To the left you can see Sam's Buick.

'54 Cadillac - Milton Melton

Customizing this '54 Cadillac for Milton Melton was a major piece of work: Milton was a supermarket executive from Beverly Hills. He called his Eldorado convertible, the "Parisienne." We sectioned 3-inches from the body through the rear fenders, hood, and top of the doors, as well as other custom bodywork. Eventually, the car went to Bohmann & Schwartz, who built the top and painted the car. When it was finished, we showed this great looking Caddy for Milton.

Above: There's nothing like taking a brand-new car and cutting it up. Here's Sam contemplating the amount of work ahead.

Right: Once Sam had scribed his cut line across the base of the firewall, he started the cut with an air-chisel. This cutting involved removing the factory air and electrical ducts so they could be repositioned lower down the firewall when the car was reassembled. Interestingly, some of the final cuts were made with an old fashioned can opener.

Left: Sam leans on the bar, while one of the Manok boys torches the cowl. Sectioning this Cad was a long and involved project. As you can see, the door posts and hinges had to be relocated downwards and the doors had to be gutted before we sectioned them.

Right: After tidying up the cut with a hammer and dolly, the cowl was dropped to its new position. Here, Sam has welded up the join and is refitting all the duct work in the firewall. We detailed this car very well, finishing off all the section joints with lead where necessary.

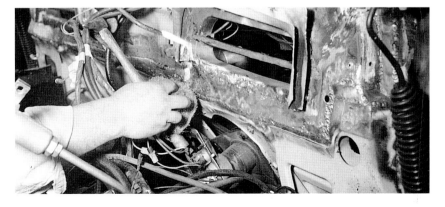

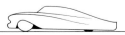

Above: The rear fenders, which had their fins removed, were extended 20 inches and ended in shotgun-style exhaust outlets built into the bumper ends.

Above Left: From this build up photo it's hard to believe that this would ever be a complete car again, but we had faith. The spare was sunk into the deck lid and mounted to the frame.

Left: Milton tries out the Cadillac, painted in primer, outside the shop.

Left: When sitting outside the Pan Pacific Auditorium alongside a stocker, you can see how long the Parisienne was. The formal landau top was made of steel over an oak buck by Schwartz.

'54 Chevrolet - Duane Steck

This '54 Chevy Bel Air hardtop custom, owned by Duane Steck, was called "Moonglow." It was a famous custom that underwent many changes over the years. It's seen here in an early rendition. Duane, who lived in Bellflower, California, was quite creative and did most of the work himself. I always enjoyed this car. From every angle it looked right with its chopped top, skirts, frenched headlights and custom grille. I also particularly remember how low it sat.

Below: Subtle changes, such as the frenched '52 Ford headlights, made Moonglow one of the show favorites. The doors, which had had their handles shaved, were opened by pressing the ribbed side trim just behind the door. The grille features ten additional grille bars.

Above: The taillights, from a '56 Chrysler, were mounted upside down into the finned fenders, described back then as "shark fins." The '56 Chevy bumper guards house backup lights in the tips. The car was painted powder blue and white to match the interior, and both Duane and Larry Watson handled the subtle pinstriping, which featured a naked woman.

'54 Ford - Top Chop

The '52-'54 Fords and Mercurys quickly became popular cars to customize, and we chopped a number of them, including this Victoria, which came to us already chopped. The chop was all wrong so to fix it, we got another roof and threw this pie chart away.

Above: From this front 3/4 photo you can see that there was quite a lot of work in this car with its deeply tunneled headlights, shaved hood, reworked grille, chopped top and altered rear fenders. Mercury quarter panels added a distinctive flair.

Above: In this rear 3/4 photo you can now see that the roof took on a more rounded shape. Notice how the window was leaned down because we couldn't cut the tempered glass.

Right: The Ford had been chopped by slicing the roof into four pieces, stretching them out to the corners, and filling the gaps. When the owner came to us, he was already in deep trouble. We threw the roof away and started over with a new one.

'54 Mercury - Ronnie Dragoo

NHRA historian Greg Sharp always said that Ronnie Dragoo of Long Beach, California, had the coolest name for a custom car guy. Ronnie also had a cool car in this '54 Mercury Monterey, which was originally owned by Dick "Peep" Jackson. Peep had a deal with Sam to chop the car in exchange for help on Sam's '52 Ford. It was a brand-new car when we cut it up, but before it was finished Peep, who drove it every day, all through construction, sold it to Ronnie. The wraparound rear window made this a difficult car to chop, but Sam soon had it figured out.

Above: There's Ronnie parked outside the house where I photographed so many customs, I often wondered what the owners thought. Incidentally, that extra door trim is from a '55 Merc, and the hubcaps are a combination of Buick and Merc parts. The way Ronnie's car was chopped gave the car a shorter passenger area but a beautiful long trunk. The rest of the car was basically stock.

Above: The car was almost brand-new when we started the chop.
An air chisel was used to remove the rear window frame complete.

Left: A hacksaw was used to cut 3 inches out of the A-pillars and 4 out of the rear before Sam and Peep lifted away the roof.

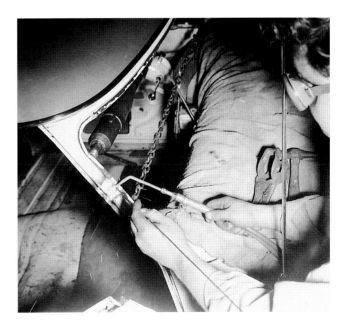

Right: Chains and a jack were used to pull the lower part of the A-pillars in and force out the upper parts while they were welded.

Left: The top half of the rear window frame was tried for position. Back then there was a lot of eyeballing of shapes and positioning as we didn't work from plans or blueprints. From this photo you can see how the glass would be leaned forward to get the shape right.

Right: Here, you can see clearly how the rear pillars were handled with the window set lower and the pillar and roof cuts shown.

'54 Mercury - "Chimbo"

We knew him only as "The Chinaman" but I nicknamed him "Chimbo" and his '54 Mercury was, unfortunately, never featured in any of the contemporary magazines because it was destroyed in the '57 fire. I did manage to photograph it before the fire. We found these two photographs and thought you might like to compare the treatment with that of Ronnie Dragoo's.

Left: As you can see in this front 3/4 photo, the Merc had a vinyl top; later, it would get an Olds bumper, quad lights and pearl paint.

Right: Chimbo's Merc shows off its skirts and new top in this shot. You can also see the round rear window fitted to the car in this photo. Unfortunately the car was in the shop, being upholstered by Roy Gilbert, when that fateful fire destroyed it.

'55 Chevrolet - Harry Hoskins

The introduction of front and rear wrap-around glass made top chopping even more difficult, and the trend began to fade somewhat toward the end of the 1950s. Nevertheless we still had work, including turning Harry's '55 into a mild custom, which was then painted white. We sliced 2-1/2 inches out of the roof and painted it candy cherry, hence its new name "The Cherry."

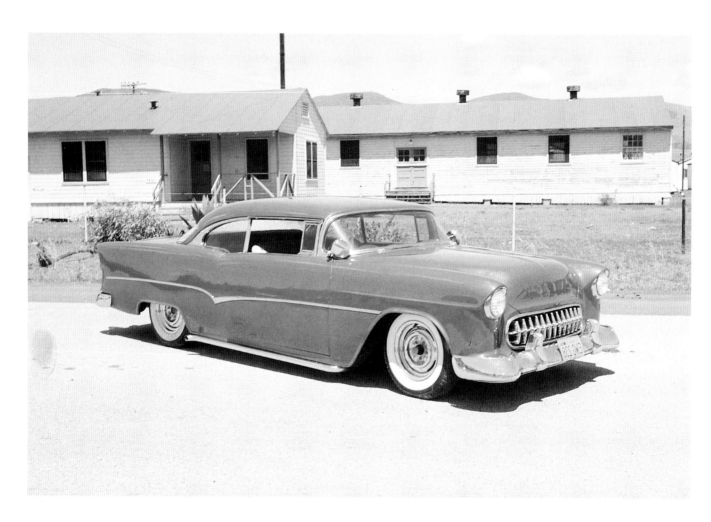

This front 3/4 photo shows the shaved and peaked hood, reformed to fit the new grille opening which houses a '56 Corvette insert. The front gravel pan was also molded and lakes pipes were added for effect. The car was painted candy cherry.

Above: The rear fenders were lengthened and peaked to house '56 Lincoln taillights, and the trunk was shaved. The rear bumper was fitted with a Pontiac license-plate guard, and the trim was from a '55 Dodge.

INDEX